Against Perfection

Publications by Richard Burns

Poetry

The Easter Rising 1967, The Restif Press, Brighton, 1968
The Return of Lazarus, Bragora Press, Cambridge, 1971
Double Flute, Enitharmon Press, London, 1972
Avebury, Anvil Press Poetry with Routledge & Kegan Paul, London, 1972;
and tr. Roberto Sanesi, La Nuova Foglio, Macerata, 1976
Inhabitable Space, John Morann, Groningen, 1976
Angels, Los Poetry Press, Cambridge, 1977, 1979, 1983
Some Poems, Illuminated by Frances Richards, Enitharmon Press, London, 1977
Learning to Talk, Enitharmon Press, London, 1980
Tree, Menard Press, London, 1980; *Tree/Arbol,* tr. Clara Janés, Papeles
de invierno, Madrid, 1986; and *Baum,* tr. T. Breuer, Kall-Sistig, 1989
Roots/Roots, Cleveland State University Poetry Center, Ohio, 1982
Black Light, Los Poetry Press, 1983, 1986; The King of Hearts, Norwich, 1995;
Crna Svetlost, tr. B. Bobić, Dečje Novine, Gornji Milovanovac, 1984;
and *Schwarzes Licht,* tr. T. Breuer, Bunte Raben Verlag, 1996
Menadzer, tr. J.B. Mišić, Writers' Association of Montenegro, 1990
Half of Nowhere, Cambridge University Press, 1998
Croft Woods, Los Poetry Press, Cambridge, 1999

Prose

Keys to Transformation, Enitharmon Press, London, 1981
Anthony Rudolf and the Menard Press, Los Poetry Press, Cambridge, 1985
Anthony Dorrell: A Memoir, St. Michael's Mount, Longstanton, 1989
With Peter Russell in Venice, 1965, University of Salzburg , 1996

Editor

An Octave for Octavio Paz (co-editor), Sceptre Press, Rushden, 1972
Ceri Richards: Drawings to Poems by Dylan Thomas,
Enitharmon Press, London, 1980
Rivers of Life, Victoria Press, Kent, 1980
In Visible Ink, Selected Shorter Poems of Roberto Sanesi, Aquila, Skye, 1983
Homage to Mandelstam (co-editor), Los Poetry Press, Cambridge, 1981
Out of Yugoslavia (co-editor), North Dakota Quarterly, 1994

RICHARD BURNS

Against Perfection

The King of Hearts
Norwich
1999

First published in 1999 by
The King of Hearts, Fye Bridge Street, Norwich NR3 1LJ

© Richard Burns 1999

ISBN 0 9518657 49

Designed and typeset in Adobe Sabon
by Marion Catlin

Cover picture: The Guitar Player by Vermeer
by permission of English Heritage Picture Library

Printed in Norwich by
BD&H Ltd

For

Lara, Gully, Jelena and Arijana

Acknowledgements

Some of these poems have appeared in or as previous books by Richard Burns: *Double Flute, Learning to Talk, Some Poems Illuminated by Frances Richards, Tree, Arbol/Tree, Roots/Routes, Black Light* and *Croft Woods*.

Several poems have been anthologised in: *Voices Within The Ark* (ed. H. Schwarz and A. Rudolf, Avon Books, New York, 1980), *New Angles* (ed. John Foster, Oxford University Press, 1987), *The Space Between* (ed. J. Walton, University of Notre Dame, Indiana, 1991), *Summoning the Sea* (ed. W. Görtschacher and G. Pursglove, University of Salzburg, 1996), *Pembroke Poets* (ed. R. Macfarlane and D. Quentin, Cambridge, 1998) and *The Mind Has Mountains* (ed. A. Holden and F. Kermode, Cambridge, 1999).

Poems have also appeared in the following magazines and journals: Equivalencias (Madrid), Lines Review (40th anniversary issue, Edinburgh, 1992), The Jewish Chronicle (London), The Jewish Quarterly (London), The Juggler (Notre Dame), Néa Estía (Athens) and Pivot (New York).

'Black is the Light' received a Duncan Lawrie Award in the Arvon Poetry Competition (1982). In an earlier, incomplete form, the sequence *The Blue Butterfly* won the H.H.Wingate – Jewish Quarterly Award for Poetry (1992).

Permission to reproduce Jan Vermeer's painting 'The Guitar Player' on the cover has been given by English Heritage.

My special thanks go to Aude Gotto. Not only was this book her idea, but she selected its contents, edited it and guided it through all stages of production. I am particularly grateful for her wholly unexpected – and extremely heartening – enthusiasm for several long poems. I should also like to thank Peter Mansfield, who gave invaluable editorial advice.

RB, Cambridge, 1999

Contents

Light beyond light. 9
Give Time. 10
Against the Day 11
Poem at the Autumn Equinox 20
Genealogy. 22
The Core 23
May. 24
After Eternity 30
Tree 31
In the room suddenly 41
Male Figure Playing a Double Flute. 43
Angels 44
Daimon's Sermon 48
God has not moved a furlong 52
Poems from *Black Light* 53
    Black is the light behind the blaze of day 53
    Volta 54
    Only the Common Miracle 56
    Shell. 58
Poems from *The Blue Butterfly* 59
    The Death of Children. 59
    The Blue Butterfly. 60
    Nada: Hope or Nothing 61
    There is scant hope 62
    Clean out the house 63
    Statement by a Survivor. 64
    Nothing is lost always 68
    The Mirror 70
Croft Woods. 71
Guests 80
Poems from *The Manager* 81
    I will speak 81
    Once, hearing music 82
    In the parks 83
Notes 85

Light beyond light
law beyond laws
stillness in flight
pulse in a pause

road of all roads
love that is higher
than all our modes
of hope or desire

show me the way
the inner eye shines
night and day
between these lines

Give Time

So take your time, enjoy it at your leisure,
Relish your hours, yet watch them pass away,
Or save time, and relinquish every pleasure
In mourning for a morning or a day,
Or, keep time, and tap out its subtle measure
Dancing in rings until steps go astray –
But give time, and receive time's finest treasure,
Visions of stars and galaxies at play.

Move through time's inner rooms and corridors,
And die imprisoned behind solid walls,
Trace each of time's results from its first cause
And hear time's hidden echoes and footfalls,
Then listen to time clapping its applause
And beg for time for extra curtain calls.

Against the Day

Against the Brydale day, which is not long . . .

To Lara, on her eighteenth birthday

I

Against the window, against desire, against
Expectation, which is not long, she leans

Away from her light source, and her eyes
Stay just in shadow as she seems to smile

Or say hello, before she starts singing
Her song which binds unguarded love to you:

Against the gold and white fire of her dress,
Against a covered, curtain-hidden sun,

She plays it throughout everlastingness,
Glowing, a pearl, offset against the day.

II

Against her covered, curtain-hidden sun,
By being just and all she knows she is,

She plays her being's pattern, as she glows
Against the day, which settles in her core

And grows there, generous, clear centred, sure,
As if she were some sturdy, dew-pearled rose

Gathering light towards her. It collects
Within her forehead, pools beneath her skin

And radiates towards us, quiet, strong,
Delicate, but untouchable, as her song.

III

This music binds unguarded love to you,
Her fingers may say to her instrument's strings

And her melody call to the shadows and gloom
And whoever listens in the next room

At the end of her gaze, we cannot see.
Hello. Hello. Are you there? Can you hear?

And whether she aims to impress or attract
Or simply to please, or just doesn't care,

It's subtle, this mooted joy she folds
In her envelope of luminous air.

IV

She is a pearl, offset against the day,
Against the twin perfection she knows she is

And the other perfection she leans towards
Which is the space gathering between us

From the pools of her densely pupilled eyes
And the few rich, perfect, ornate things

In the room where, smiling, she sits and sings
The silence which frets our history's

Lacunae in unheard of, guessed at bars,
And lights against the space she occupies.

V

Delicate, but untouchable as her song,
In playing, she tunes an orchestrated light

Which is her being's pattern, and no more
Than what she is, or has awareness of.

Smiling, she plays as if her song were willed
By a more intelligent, kinder love

Protecting and surrounding her young face
Than any we have understanding of,

As if the day itself had overspilled
Itself through her to make those fingers skilled.

VI

In her envelope of luminous air,
Joy may be folded, and some other things:

Pearls round her neck, but no bracelets or rings,
Whose absence may mean, imply or suggest

An innocence: in her ringleted hair,
Ermine and silk, she is wearing her best,

As she plays on, quiet, aware-unaware
And ready to move yet still seem at rest,

Whether she's smiling, or blushing, or sings
And plays for herself, and just doesn't care.

VII

She lights against the space she occupies,
Familiar in its elegance and grace,

And yet, in youthful eagerness, her face
Leans still against more space, she may not know

Outside this screened, framed room she's captured in
Against the daylight, closeted for good

In the too pure perfection of a pearl,
Against desire, that radiates through her skin:

Now, now, she plays, for she is young, a girl
Just turning from us into womanhood.

VIII

The day in her, to make her fingers skilled
(As though she were the space she occupies)

To reach across the broken, varnished years
In silent music no-one really hears

Towards us in another century,
Has made her human: no pure pearl or bloom

Could possess such composure. Those deep eyes
Are burdened with too fine, alert intelligence

And too prepared, in willing mute obedience
To wait forever in her drawing room.

IX

If she plays for herself, and just doesn't care
Whose being she plucks from her instrument's strings

(Woman, girl, woman, in yellow and white),
But smiles at an audience of none, in the wings,

No secret admirer, protected from sight,
No parent or guardian to applaud her, or call,

Then it's her own selfhood she sifts as she sings
And her own self-becoming wavering there

Hidden against the chiaroscuro half-light
As in an unseen mirror on a wall.

X

Just turning from us into womanhood
Against the day, against parental praise,

She gives to shadows one half of her face
And a warm human longing fills her gaze

Yet quietens it, for it is still uncertain.
So, balanced between action and repose,

She looks away. What there she sees or knows
Offstage, in her own private, secret place,

Waits there, without embodiment or history
and is not for the telling. It's her mystery.

XI

To wait for ever in her drawing room
Could be her destiny, always: poised steady

As a dart to pierce the adulthood
She leans against, but never will command

More than the brush held in her maker's hand
Who formed her, against day, against desire

And against his day's possessions. Against
Her bridal day, no girl could seem so ready

As she, in certain hope, so qualified
By all but nature, for her womanhood.

XII

As if glimpsed in a mirror on a wall
She's posed, as ornamental as the tree

Gilt-framed behind her: nature trapped inside
Artifice, inside artifice, where she,

Pearled tracery on rich parental pride,
Sits screened in flattened space, to play on three

Dimensions, self-contained, in perfect liberty:
But the fourth, our common history, we share

With her across the barricaded years
Within whose space alone may she be freed.

XIII

What is not for the telling, but her mystery,
We cannot know: she may play for her groom,

Or entertain a friend, or family guest,
Who, deep in the interior of her room,

Off in the wings, unfettered by her frame,
Knows her full repertoire we cannot hear.

We only see her hopeful gaze arrest
On absent presence, distant and yet near,

And whoever may be listening, manifest
Space as the sound her silent song must claim.

XIV

From all in nature must her womanhood
Remain exempt, unless you hear her. This

Is still and always all art ever meant,
And only you have natural power to call

Her being from its painted artifice
Created by the man who patterned all

He knew in her, of love's integument
Against the day. You are the instrument

She plays on, until doomsday: against you
The gloom she gazes, still and always, through.

XV

Within whose space, alone, may she be free
If not in yours? Come, hear her subtle playing

Unlock the solid shutters of the years
And open them, light-wrought, in filigree:

Playing her being's pattern, she plays true.
She is the song she plays, and what it's saying

(This music wings unguarded love to you),
Calls you, who are her song's recipient,

Yourself, to pattern love, her music's key,
And join her in the gift of this, her moment.

XVI

Your space: the single sound her song may claim
To open, is the gift a father knew

Seeing his natural daughter come of age.
This child of his will meet her adulthood

By playing her being's pattern quietly through
The centuries, until she reaches you.

You are her hope, her natural heritage.
You are the absent audience in her wings.

Your entrance is the cue a parent would
Most desire for her. It is for you she sings.

XVII

The gloom she gazes still and always through
Clears, as you listen. This, her painter knew:

Unless you hear her music, and impress
The sound it makes upon your inner ear,

She will not play at all but wait forever.
She gives herself. Her gift is its own giver

And its envelope of luminous air
Bears your mark on it. You are its address.

Whoever you may be, although unknown,
Her music plays to all of you alone.

XVIII

Come, join her in the gift of this, her moment,
Becoming her own secret audience

As if you were the listener in the wings
For whom her music's made, performed and meant,

And, though this be impossible, confess
How well you hear and understand these songs

She plays to you through everlastingness
On soundless subtle chords no aural sense

Could ever pluck, except against the heart,
Against the day, against desire, in art.

Poem at the Autumn Equinox

For Arijana

Returning dreams. The one about falling
and the one about a house
owned and lived in but never fully explored
and the one containing a word
clearly heard and recognised
from a language unknown,
which I can never pronounce. Now you have gone
let them take me over. I am their island
willing to be drowned.

After the end of falling, you will come to a river
and walk beside it along a worn footpath
bordered by nettles and willows.
In the house you will find a room
and in the room a mirror,
and in the mirror a portrait of a girl dressed in leaves,
golden and green, and in her hand a wand.
After the word and the deaths of its many echoes
first you will hear a silence strike like a gong
and then from the silence another voice emerge,
and that is the voice to listen to,
that is the voice to follow. The girl
who enters the room and looks out of her mirror
stands on the tide and her wand is the rainbow.

The voice arrives on the tide but is no part of it
and if it seems to belong wholly to the sea
or if it seems to belong wholly to the wind
or if its substance seems partially made of cloud,
reflections, falling leaves, or invisible splinters of light,
do not be mistaken by the sweetness of appearances.

The path leads to cliffs where butterflies and bees
play the summer long, and night is full of stars.
The girl who stands on the tide against a white horizon.
has turned into a willow framed against the sky,
and her wand which was the rainbow has spiralled away
on wings, migrating south for winter. Nothing is left
but emptiness – except for the voice. And the voice
cannot stop singing now, and all you have to do
is burn its sound in your heart and treasure it there forever.

Genealogy

For Peter and Eva Mansfield

I have come back to the orchard and a blue silence has fallen on me.
A child's swing hangs from branches in a walled and shaded corner
And a moment's curling breeze sways ripening fruit, lifts leaves,
Ruffles ferns and lilies, clusters long underlying grasses. A scent
Of something wild and beautiful, like the passing breath of God,
Lingers in its wake. I no longer know how I arrived here
Or along what path or paths. Two windows from a far house
Blaze briefly, twice, in whiteness, and shoot late afternoon sunlight
Back at me here in shadow, as somebody opens and closes them.
In a language not mine yet known, a woman's voice calls out
The name of a girl I recognise from faded sepia photographs.
Three times she calls, with a breath between each naming,
And I have shrunk to crouching and wish I were invisible,
And the girl who was nowhere darts from a tree behind me
And places her small hands over my eyelids and giggles.
She turns me around to face her, smiles the wicked smile
Shared only by children, raises forefinger to pursed lips
And turns and skips to the voice in the distant awaiting house.

The Core

I cannot bite the day to the core

It is always impossible, if half-achieved,
But never completely satisfying or satisfactory,
The return, through memory, to the wiped out
Childhood, razed city, obliterated garden
Sandwiched between Once-Upon-A-Time Street
And Never-Ever Avenue, both lined with plane trees
Whose greeny bark you used to flake and peel
Playing Hide-and-Seek on the way home from school
In a quiet suburb called Used To, Once,
The last stop, then, on the metro. It is always
Impossible, the approach, the gate clicking behind you,
Then the crunchy walk up the well-gravelled drive
And round past the lilac between kitchen door and garage
Into that safe green protected space
Where the ground is littered with fallen apples
And the swing dangles from leafy branches
Emptied of its child, as if just emptied,
And the voice of a familiar adult, now dead,
Is heard from the patio by the French windows
Calling that child's name, calling, recalling,
Echoing across the chasm of decades,
With the ululation of syllables, the precise inflections
And gentle authoritative tone of a voice
Unrecognisable. To peel back
The strata of years and despairs, skin the fruit
Of time, bite through to its ripe pulp, unveil
Its core, is impossible, and you, we, I always fail.

May

As I walk in the garden with Lara and Alexander,
Between the dying lilac and opening, first rose,
The air belongs to summer again, and longing.
Pink blossoms are browning and falling. It's May.
The world anoints my whole body in glory,
But I'm not drunk on you yet, world, although I'm trying,
Knocking each breath back like a double brandy
Because your body's beauty strikes terror through me,
As death blows through the fences, spreading pollen,
And, because my brain keeps back and shoulders firm
Against the walls I have built around old sadnesses,
Because it thinks becauses, barred in ironies,
And now, as the walls inside me slowly melt,
I don't know where they've gone, the fears I knew
For years and years, and trusted more than gladness,
And want, at once, and do not want this melting
And terror that fall together with blossoms falling,
My poem tries harder not to betray its pain.

Now I'll make you a poem, from lilac, I want
To tell my children. A true story. Lara holds my hand
And Alexander bobs, cradled in the nook of my arm.
Fthah, says Lara, pointing. Does she mean *There*
Or *Flower*? And the whole garden opens around her,
You can see it in her wide eyes, as, two years old,
Cheeks burning, she toddles to the brink of speech.
And this precise instant, I know I shall remember
The instant itself fixed forever, when we shared the world

Whole, in a word, and know also the act of knowing,
Hers and mine joined together, will be that memory's core,
Far finer formed than in dream time, seen clearer
Than in a photograph. Hairs on my forearms stand,
Tears brim in my eyes, I shiver in the warmth,
My fantasies are earthed, and all love is fleshed.
And now, the garden opens its soul to me also,
And its whole complex world, like a perfect jar, cracks,
Spilling into my head a poem scented with lilac.

Here, children, your poem. But my voice sticks. I say
Nothing. The poem's words, unspoken, are too full of pain.
Wrong. Wrong. Lies. The pain in the poem is mine.
This is the month my father broke his heart in.
It cracked. He died. The lilac was in bloom.
In the back room of our quiet North London house
Whose French windows opened on another garden,
Israel Alexander Berengarten, musician,
Born in Warsaw, brought up in the East End,
Singer in seven languages, including Yiddish,
Each evening through that spring had played his cello
Till long past dark, in tears, his finest concert,
To his daughter Sarah, born deaf, dumb and blind,
To get her to hear, to try to get her to hear
The song of the Swan of Tuonela
Moving out through silence over the Black Lake.
Israel Alexander, I'm calling you back in this poem
I want the courage to give my children.

Blind, deaf and speechless to the world, making high-pitched
Raucous screams, like an owl, or an owl's prey,
With lolling head, lips drooling, her arms
Flailing, contorted, fingers unable to clutch,
His mindless infant daughter broke his spirit.
And one May morning, his forty-sixth birthday,
He stayed in bed, with chest cramps, back pains, toothache,
Grumbling at Rosalind, again six months pregnant
And suffering morning sickness, to answer the doorbell.
A telegram, with flowers. Many Happy Returns.
She waddled back upstairs bearing the light greeting,
But he lay there dead, and one day later
She buried him with his cello bow beside him.
As in a dream, as clear, as in a photograph,
I see his writhing mouth, I hear him calling
Through a morning sleek and pregnant with ephemeral
Perfume of lilac on the pollen-laden air
And all his thoughts and vessels stop at once.

Now Rosalind sits at her mirror combing out her hair,
Hollow-eyed, big-bellied, in a loose smock and slippers,
While her four-year-old son studies her through the glass.
Mummy, he asks, Tell me, when's Daddy coming home?
Quietly she answers, He won't come back. He's dead.
Soon you'll have new baby to play with instead.
And, slowly, as a bow moves over a cello's strings
Playing some old lament, she goes on combing her hair
Whose delicate perfume reminds the boy of lilac.

Then a girl is born, Alexis. More telegrams. More flowers.
A clan of smiles fills the house. Aunts, uncles, cousins.
Only the empty O of a wooden unplayed instrument
Howls still in silence in a corner against the wall.
Israel Alexander – the Greek means Defender of Men,
The boy is soon to learn – will not return again.
Now, thirty years later, Rosalind sleeps by her husband
On the other side of his bow, and Sarah too is dust,
And the aunts and uncles lie low, buried or cremated.

Genealogy and mourning: the language of the Jews.
Ada came, and Alec, Gertrude, and big-souled Bertha,
Dave with his fat cigar and a half-crown for the boy,
Lily, Jacques and Harry, Annie, Rita and Stanley,
Huge-hearted Manny, Bessie, and Renée, Frank's wife:
To name each plant that grows, each individual stem
That blossomed, fruited, died, and in turn was seeded
Here, in memory's garden, and to forget not one,
Is my task and possession, I want to explain
To my children. But still, my voice sticks, and the poem
I wanted to make them and their children's children,
My own accurate testimony of what I knew and loved,
To last, if not forever, longer than my own life,
Falters on my tongue, as pain pulls my breath back still.
What need they know of this knowledge, or understand
Of this heritage, this litany of sadnesses
Borne on the lilac's perfume, whispering through my mind,
Where, from every bloom in this garden, I hear ghosts?

Now, walking in this garden, among blossoms falling,
With my own daughter Lara and son Alexander,
I hear my father's music call me from his grave,
And the Swan of Tuonela rises from the lake
To beat its white wings against my shuttered heart.
How shall these dead be honoured, let alone counted?
I ask of the song, and my father's cello replies:
Lilac has newly fallen. Now is the time of roses.
Wake from your dream. Speak out, to men's hearts and minds.
Wake, and walk out, now, free, into the world
Where now your small son coos and babbles as he rides
Across this May garden in the crook of your arm
As though you were a chariot he turns like a God
Over a Greek heaven, and like another Maev, new risen,
Your two-year-old daughter herself culls speech from flowers.
Defender of Men, I reply, Here, in this poem
I wanted to make right and stammered long to speak,
Play again for the born, and the unborn children.

Here, poem, begin, while still these dream images
Are manifest around me, and each one, like a bee,
Collects unnumbered memories into my brain cells,
Gently ushered and hosted by perfumes from flowers,
And, heavy among these houses, fences, walls and wires,
Across these English gardens, along these neat avenues
Lined with privet and hawthorn, I hear the air hum
With sounds of a deep instrument being stroked unseen
By my father's bow, plucked seasoned from his coffin,

Its fibres rubbed silken on the resin of my thought.
I want that sound of his big-bellied cello
With strings well tautened, strong and finely tuned,
Rooted and resonant, here, in my poem,
Till its chords, huge-hearted, burst as a tree bursts
Open in leaf and flower, weaving, interweaving
On air, the scents of summer, lilac and roses,
To shower joy on my children, Lara and Alexander,
And honey of memory be savoured on their tongues.

And here, since love has called me to speak out
Across years, through pain, to celebrate in the quiet
Words of a poem made in a garden, for children,
The music my father made, amid lilac perfume,
I want that same scent, of sweet almost unbearable
Promise of summer, to drown my own self-doubt,
My hard-edged ironies and soft-centred cowardice
With its living body's presence, and so thoroughly
To permeate every filament of this poem
That every word in it will radiate his love.
So now, the poem ends, as *Fthah*, my daughter calls,
In an instant that echoes and shimmers, and the spines
Of trees tremble, and a hush falls over the garden,
And this thing, or process, or movement, pours molten
In the well of a word, where it will go on ringing,
Spanned by fragile speech, firmed and bell-like always,
Impossible to break and made doubly deep and strong
By my father's music which called me from his grave.

After Eternity: a dialogue

For Catherine Ng

First there was void, and then a cosmic bang.
Time is an arrow, not a boomerang.
Life is a knotted string time pulls out straight,
Woven by change and chance into your fate.

While swallows gather and the summer dies
Love is wiped out like summer butterflies.
But true love lasts for ever, never trying,
Never striving or dying, time defying.

After eternity, we live out time.
The bell rings but you cannot hear the chime.
We live to praise, to celebrate and treasure
Infinite moments that no clock can measure.

The lock is timeless and the hands are yours
To turn the keys that open all time's doors.

Tree

The tree of life groweth with slow and steady increase through unmeasured time

Tree planted
  in my core
spreading growing
  tree of songs
many branched
  flame tree
rooted in death
  blood bathed
breath blown
  bone fibred
body tree
  elemental
tree in a seed
  full throated
thousand tongued
  thick skinned
creaking tree
  enduring thunder
wind eroded
  snow bound
survivor tree
  skeletal
under storm clouds
  budding slow
through despair
  thrusting hopes
of high skies
  cirrus strewn
milky ways
  and birds returning

wakening
   sleep laden tree
circled in memories
   close grained
springwood
   and summerwood
tree of dreams
   and visitations
leaved with hair
   of fallen heroes
snake wreathed
   giant guarded
threaded with voices
   and children's laughter
ancestor tree
   earth drinking
sky swallowing
   bowelled living
grave tree
   light eating
pillar of wisdom
   of smoke of cloud
desert beacon
   whorled tornado
fire fountain
   golden chain
leading the way
   through night
with agate jet
   and haematite
from evening
   gathering emerald
carnelian
   and diamond dews
and in the studded
   bowl of dawn
with pearl and opal
   dissolving them

spreadeagled
  against the morning
a scented trellis
  spanning noon
blue crowned
  tree of earth
water fire
  of air of airs
light ship
  dusky barge
sailing on
  wind seasoned
around year ends
  and back again
clay moored
  soil harboured tree
prow lapped
  by heaven's tides
sun cradle
  moon basket
cloud blanketed
  cask of stars
rocking meteors
  shaking planets
ploughing galaxies
  on long oars
world hammering
  sky raking
word breaking
  rocksplitting tree
bonecracking
  wrist of boughs
tower of strength
  pivot fulcrum
axial roof tree
  probing pharos
ever turning
  clawed through crust

of cliff and crag
   pointed dactyl
spark igniting
   flame hurling
quill clutched
   in a stone fist
illuminating
   day's page
in green and gold leaf
   manuscript
chiselling plaques
   in night's crypt
with serifs inked
   in baryons
kindling speech
   of origins
to sing darkness's
   molten core
of ice
   moss and coal
fossil fern
   and dinosaur
time tree
   revolving burning
prising open
   history's lips
drilling its jaws
   to spit pips
needle twigs
   and wiry shoots
earthed in its seams
   and blood routes
ore flowers
   on brittle stems
magnetic amber
   diadems
electric tree
   lightning conductor

energy funnel
   through stratospheres
chimney built
   in the pot of death
fuelling years
   with quiet breath
tree of creation
   tree of destruction
temple planted
   in an upturned skull
worming woody
   fibres through
eye socket
   and mandible
world tree
   scroll keeping
cave covered
   by sky mountain
joy tent pitched
   in wilderness
dome whispering
   spire trembling
gargoyle gnarled
   buttress of hills
glory cone
   mist piercing
latticed steeple
   nesting angels
fan vaulted
   echoing tree
runged ladder
   for the soul's fingers
valved throat
   winged glottis
ringing singing
   ribcage tree
harmonising
   forest airs

and air of plains
   in symphony
with the unceasing
   ocean fend
orchestral baton
   dowser's rod
dipping bending
   greenwood sapling
bowed by longing
   flex of hope
tightrope stretched
   from loam to God
tuned wand
   alembic
caduceus twined
   branching vessel
thermometer measuring
   ages' heat
mercurial sap
   rising falling
hollow tree
   fluted with stomata
wooden well
   mine tunnelled
bell cord
   and lungs of Hades
gale harness
   fanning the damned
and the twice dead
   and the never born
with harp tinkling
   in glen and glade
and lament of orchards
   for Hesperides
womb tree
   moist lipped
rain collecting
   underground tree

resin caulked
  wine vat
tree of desire
  taboo fruited
mountain spring
  orgy scented
waterfall
  weeping tree
flooded river
  magma breasted
lava tree
  sowing islands
eddying delta
  coral tree
perpetually blazing
  deciduous
tree of madness
  tree of passion
set with thorns
  sweating blood
pain tree
  evergreen
showering ghosts
  shedding children
common tree
  brittle old
crowded stunted
  overshadowed tree
insect gnawed
  rot infected
lightning blasted
  husk of famine
raped mutilated
  people's tree
obelisk
  dead tree
uprooted felled
  sawn plank

hearth tree
  for warmth and fuel
table tree
  for bread and wine
architraved
  thyrsus totem
bound and staked
  earthed and fused
blood spattered
  royal trunk
nailing hell
  to paradise
gallows tree
  rising again
knuckled knotted
  blind man's staff
swordblade
  heavy hilted
thick boled
  ivory tusk
ebony spear
  erect conquering
tree in a prairie
  in a city garden
pruned and tended
  by patient hands
quiet tree
  of yes of no
of this of that
  of black of white
confluence
  of pasts and futures
rooted in ever
  praising now
flesh tree
  rimmed in muscle
blood and sweat
  sighing shivering

shuddering tree
  generous
sperm tree
  life pump
everbrimming
  around whose roots
the serpent coils
  around whose branches
flits the white bird
  tree of spirits
tree of secrets
  buried in heaven
to flower through veins
  arteries nerves
capillary tree
  meristematic
your tap root drowned
  in infinite skies
I descend up
  and ascend down
rod of aeons
  of Adam Kadmon
Jesse David
  and Sataniel
and Moses
  on the high mountain
Buddha tree
  Tilopa tree
zen tree
  tantric tree
Kali's tree
  dancing on skulls
volcanic tree
  of Ashtaroth
Lilith
  Ishtar and Astarte
nurturing
  moss and lichen

mould gathering
   mushroom tree
mother of orchids
   and mistletoe
tree of Dryads
   tree of Druids
where the spider weaves
   and the rooks nest
and the bat flitters
   and the kestrel waits
tree of lives
   of consciousness
generative
   language tree
speaking names
   telling stories
histories
   transformations
depthless tree
   deathless tree
tree of comrades
   of airs I breathe
unpruned
   untameable
immortal tree
   overarching
freedom tree
   tree of love
tree of justice
   human rainbow
blossoming

In the room suddenly

In the room suddenly everything went
　　　Very still and quiet. There was no space
For knowledge on display or its acknowledgement.
　　　One open look shone out of every face
And into every other, in amazement.
　　　It came without announcement, without trace,
And everyone was silent for a moment
　　　In wholly naked truthfulness and grace.

Not beauty, quite, if beauty is a sheen
　　　Holding its beholders in a steady state
Of trance. Nor did it mean or seem to mean
　　　Anything words or concepts could translate.
Breathing just went on normally. No screen
　　　Or veil was drawn from eyes to shower a spate
Of revelations through us, and no paean
　　　Of angel voices shook from heaven's gate.

If beauty, though, is constancy of presence
　　　That stays on, song-like, through its own transitions,
Into a singing quietness as dense
　　　As after a concert, by skilled musicians,
Despite what follows, more talk, more pretence,
　　　More wit lined up behind old inhibitions,
Then it was beauty, of the seventh sense,
　　　Defying reasons, flouting definitions.

We knew. We were not fools. Description fails,
　　　For gaps in time like these defy defining.
They are too dense, perception's loaded scales
　　　Tip to silence's dark side, intertwining
Whatever seems, flows past, forgets and pales,
　　　Into a sort of sound there, like a whining
For heaven in the head, for frayed details
　　　To gather there, connecting and combining.

I fail. This fades. Its skein breaks too. I know.
    But who will mend the lovely broken chain
That garlands all things, years hence or ago,
    And fits such timeless jewels to our pain,
Unless by metamorphosis we grow
    Seeds from that moment's core back in the brain?
That sudden silent order was: although
    Order be lost, rejoice. Begin again.

Male Figure Playing a Double Flute

National Museum, Athens

In austere polished marble, Orpheus plays,
his flute clamped tight between untiring jaws,
immune to criticism, deaf to praise,
transcending censure, wonder or applause.

With those twin pipes stuck in that chinless face
he played the first tune Asia ever heard,
and smuggled it to Europe out of Thrace:
he plays it now, though we don't hear a word.

His arms are poised like handles of some urn
that held a script which spelt the name divine,
but we who puzzle out its script to learn
that ageless secret, cannot read a line.

The long proud lifted neck, unleashed in leaping
from the four footed posture of the beast,
signals the world that Europe's soul is sleeping
and mind has not yet dawned upon the East.

Erect, yet legs like haunches, feet like paws,
his thighs primeval tree trunks turned to stone,
bridges from mind's inquiry and earth's laws
to silence that's immortal and alone.

He plays himself: there is no other song
behind those eyes, half closed in ecstasy,
but the same trial through all the ages long,
the erring spirit rising over entropy.

Angels

We were a multitude, until the hunters,
scouting the immemorial pastures
with hewn weapons, on foot and horseback,
tracked us down where we ambled grazing
and fell upon us with poisoned javelins,
picking us off, first one by one,
then scourging by hundreds as they closed in,
burning, smoking us from the homelands,
hounds baying, snapping our heels,
till, blood-glutted, gorged on our meat,
wearing our hides, copying our calls
and rubbing our fat, death-scented,
into their flesh to charm and ensnare us,
in droves ambushed, for blood smell only,
as if to wipe out a hunger for hunger
by slaughtering, to become us, to be us,
their glazed eyes deep, ice-covered pools
where our charred valleys were drained moistureless
and our own murders measured and mirrored,
and we scattered to barren tundra.
And there evolved. In full light and day ebb
and utter darkness, warily through every
season, kept watch, and by winds smelled them,
learned their shadow shapes and cunning
and when to rush through the closed circles
of their web-knit formations that hemmed us in
amid moving henges of hurlers and missiles
and, leaner, hardened, lighter-footed,

wove secret speech of our own.
But on they harried us, overtaking
infants and aged as they fell back,
hacked off limbs, and what was left
of crippled mutilated bodies
hanged for trophies on bark-stripped poles,
while we who still had strength enough
fled through the few remaining trees,
stumbled aimless over moors and heathland
into deserts to die of thirst, hid
in caves and were lost in their windings
under bleak hills, or perished in forests
beyond borders of the known world rim.
We who survived, ten, twelve, sixteen,
now wild in willpower and aware of destiny,
waking more sternly with each weary step,
came out of despair and to land edge
and plunged for refuge in deep waters
under the ice floes. And six or seven died
frozen or drowned, and there were no more
young. Lungs afire for want of air,
the rest swallowed, held on, swam deeper,
limbs attuning to water's rhythms,
building fat under newly sealed pores,
muscles till now unused growing firmer,
breath longer, blood beat slower,
the whole skin another ear drum,
eyes widening to take in darkness.

Self-delighting in a borrowed world,
slow to learn grace, we received as a rite
water's gift, laughter, that drowns weeping
and engulfs memory of all time but presence
which, itself a flood, buoyed us up
to sing across aeons, and our long calls
spanned oceans' depths and embraced the other
depths we embraced in and through one another,
till our speech took on the pitch and resonance
memory's currents had eroded in us
wound round the endless whorls of the sea.
And so multiplied, grew sleek and lazy,
vast in girth, living only for music,
when their sensors picked up our frequencies.
Then slaughter was unstinted and our cries,
churning placid waters, hammering the soft
inverted womb the seas had become, whose walls
we beat on, numbing last strengths uselessly,
jammed their tracking instruments as too late
remembering a nightmare from another
world, or other existence, again we woke
and dragged their bucking vessels leashed behind us
across the waves' vertiginous surface. Then blood
stained estuaries and caked whole coastlines
where our hauled wrecks were carved and heaped
in messes on the beaches, till the creeks stank.
Then we were few: three, perhaps, four.
To zones unhaunted, by no fish followed,

where water's weight and sheer blackness
pressed till we shrank and merged with shadows,
down we dived, deeper than terror.
Then we were two, and we sang each other
of Tiphareth, of the Throne, of the Glory.
Indescribable our lamentations,
we, the uncounted, the unaccountables,
sons and daughters of the starry heavens
become a lost calling without a name
drifting among unfathomed valleys,
until I called, recalled, and heard
no answering song. Then quietly I climbed
and on a still sea trumpeted, took air
and dived for ever. And you'll not find me
nor you nor you, till the almond tree flowers
on the mountain, and there is no more sea.

Daimon's Sermon

"I have kept faith, I have kept faith,"
    In sleep I mutter, toss and groan,
As, through my dream, a white robed wraith
    Accosts me, "Liar, to the bone!

You have betrayed the names of Man,
    Your destiny, and the true word."
I answer him as best I can:
    "I tell you, this is just absurd."

Closer he stalks. "You still betray
    Life, which you never merited,
Wasting your mother's gift away,
    Yourself have disinherited,

For you are profligate in love,"
    He hisses. Though I cringe and shake
And stand at bay, I do not move.
    God, am I dreaming or awake?

"I am the core of darkness come
    With shadows here to wrap you round,"
He laughs, "and I shall strike you dumb."
    Still I stand rooted to the ground.

"I have kept faith. At least, I've tried,"
    Blushing, I hear myself insist.
I won't give in. I have some pride.
    But now he grasps me by the wrist

And hurls me, broken, on the floor.
    I curl there, foetus-like, and weep,
"I just can't take it any more."
    He sneers, "Poor fish, go back to sleep."

He watches as I lose control.
    "It's all gone rotten, all a mess.
I've lost my heart, I've lost my soul."
    He snickers, "You deserve no less."

I hold my breath, pretend I'm dead.
    I'll never let it go again.
It sprouts a cancer in my head
    Which threads its pathways through my brain.

"Body, become a sunken hull
    In which all human hopes lie drowned.
My skin, be barnacled, my skull
    A cave where fishes swim around."

I thrash at them - "Let me alone!"
    But each one slips between my hands.
I'm drowning, falling like a stone,
    Life drains from blood and nerves and glands.

I care but do not care. I damn
    My friends and loves. "My life is cursed."
He laughs, "Great acting! What a sham!
    Badly performed, though well rehearsed."

Between hands' grilles, out of one eye,
    I see his shadow, and explode.
I writhe, I moan, "Please, let me die."
    I call him leech, bat, vulture, toad.

I spit. I scratch. I scream. I rage.
    I mess myself. Yes, let him see!
And let me see if he'll assuage
    The fullness of my misery.

Silence around, silence inside,
    Twin echoes of deep loneliness.
Slowly I open both eyes wide.
    No blood. No vomit. Emptiness.

Slowly I draw a deep breath.
    I ask, "Who are you? What's your name?
Slowly words form: "Who nourisheth
    His daimon feedeth life's own flame."

Slowly I crawl onto my knees,
    Heaving and lurching. Yet I stand.
Though no-one's there, my spirit sees
    An angel take me by the hand.

I blink. What angel? No-one's there!
    But I breathe, alive from head to feet.
"The world is yours and mine to share,"
    A voice inside me, soft and sweet,

Whispers. I recognise it's mine.
    The wraith was me! And every voice
I heard inside me - all were mine!
    And now they sing, "Go now. Rejoice.

Sow joy in word and joy in deed.
    Sow joy in soil of human need.
Sow joy in beauty. Plant the seed.
    And from your love, let more joy breed."

God has not moved a furlong

God has not moved a furlong
or an inch since last time eyes saw him.
The birds are word perfect in their bird song
and have no need of rehearsal
while you and I stammer out little fabricated poems.

There are no dead. They walk
the air we sing.
It's not the hills we have to move
but domes of ashes in the mouth.

Poems from *Black Light*

Black is the light behind the blaze of day

Angelic and black, light . . .
Angelic and black, day . . .

Black is the light behind the blaze of day,
Your summons comes, clear from the angel's throat.
The sun's black horses call your heart away.

Though bright the stain of dawn upon the bay
Which in celestial ink its author wrote,
Black is the light behind the blaze of day.

Though morning's cloudy mares are dappled grey
With rainbow mane and many coloured coat,
The sun's dark horses call your heart away.

Their riders gallop by. Too swiftly they
Will trample down the shades noon kept afloat.
Black is the light behind the blaze of day.

Night's chariot approaches, Don't delay.
Haul evening's golden gate up. Cross the moat.
The sun's dark horses call your heart away.

You scent that whinnying wind? The horses neigh.
You see it now? You hear that perfect note?
Black is the light behind the blaze of day.
The sun's dark horses call your heart away.

Volta

. . . now that dusk falls . . .

King sun, rosy cheeked, day's sovereign coin,
you touch me, and my skin becomes a cornea,
my spine an optic nerve, and my body trembles
half dazzled by the pool of gold you pour
over this sea and city, and I'm blinded.
Here once stood rows – and still I know they stand –
of houses and streets, belonging to another city,
not this one you have utterly transformed.

We walk along the waterfront. The night
fishermen's boats are ready to set out,
motors chugging, paraffin lamps in the bows,
and the whole town's out for the promenade,
lovers arm in arm, and young men swaggering,
mothers and fathers, children eating ice-cream,
old men watching from tables at pavement cafés,
and the darkening hills move closer, like friendly animals.

Sweet evening skyglow, spread on hills and bay,
your arm grazes mine now, as if by accident,
like the touch of this young woman who walks beside me
with heavy hips, small steps and swinging gait,
jet hair swept back, delicate throat and shoulders
deep summer bronzed, and her olive brown laughing.
I drink you, shimmering light, like wine, like music,
as her ancestors have drunk you thousands of years.

Porous city, her name is *Eleftería,*
and though your scars are grey flecks in her eyes,
still, at this hour when light and light's inflections
play subtly in her face as speech or song,
hers is the ancient right to walk this quayside
as instrument and guardian of your light,
collecting it in the wells of her deep pupils,
and hers, the darling freedom, to tread you like a dancer.

Darling evening light thousands of years old,
clear throated singer, lovely as this woman,
how can I not adore the grace you cast
this city and its people in, a mould
that sculptures all it touches, the whole world?
I have become your slave, if not your citizen.
And thirsting to drink you wholly, I would fill
every pore with your radiance, her freedom.

Only the Common Miracle

. . . between your face and your face . . .

It isn't much to ask, only the common miracle, in the silent speech of
　　lovers, the way I want to talk
to you, and you to me, is only a small sight away from angelic
　　voices pouring out of blue skies without a single cloud
when you turn round and wonder who spoke to you but nobody's
　　there
except on your left the same dusty track and the dry grass with the
　　single fig tree in the field
and beyond its stone walls, the mountain and on your right, the sea;

or when you stand astonished, in a street in some foreign city,
　　thinking you heard a friend
greet you in your own language, someone very familiar once, you
　　haven't seen for years
with the same old voice, laughing, playful, perhaps even slightly
　　ironic,
and everything you had forgotten suddenly clears before you in
　　the naked morning light, as the blood rushes to your head
and you forget your errand, the traffic stops, and the buildings start
　　whirling about you;

or when, at passion's crest you open your eyes a moment to keep
    resurrection at bay
and between the face of the person you love and the face of the
    person you love
another face appears on the wave you've never seen before but
    always have known and will know
and a gap opens for a voice, which isn't yours or mine, but we both
    hear quite clearly, and recognise,
and understand, and adore, because you know as well as I do, my
    love, that it's your voice, not mine;

it's not much to ask, only the common miracle, but people like
    you and me have been travelling
like this for years, along the same dirt track through the same city
    streets the same weary beds,
foreign in our own country, no longer recognising the speech of
    men or women we know, of our own flesh,
So how then can we be expected to converse with angels or even
    with old friends, long dead,
let alone speak the language of love, let alone the language of love?

Shell

Still there remains the yellow essence, summer . . .

The golden giant shell hangs nailed against your wall, more than a little cracked, though you mended it with glue, and drilled two clean holes there for memory's green cord to loop through, and hammered the nail in firmly to make sure it wouldn't fall. Summer has shrunk and dried to an ornament in the hall, souvenir of some place you passed or name you thought you knew, which, like a tarnished mirror, no longer quite shows true, except when faded sea scents come to your recall. Then suddenly the mirror no longer shows your face, but hands enclosing hands over a pebble on a beach, and medusas, starfish, and seagreens, delicate as lace, and an underwater statue of a blonde youth, out of reach, who still may move in dance for you, perfect in poise and grace, and hail you, who have half forgotten, in the sea's secret speech.

Poems from *The Blue Butterfly*

The Death of Children

It is the death of children most offends
Nature and justice. No use asking why.
What justice is, nobody comprehends.

What punishment can ever make amends?
There's no pretext, excuse or alibi.
It is the death of children most offends.

Whoever offers arguments pretends
To read fate's lines. Although we must swear by
What justice is, nobody comprehends

How destiny or chance weaves. Who defends
Their motives with fair reasons tells a lie.
It is the death of children most offends.

Death can't deserve to reap such dividends
From these, who scarcely lived, their parents cry.
What justice is, nobody comprehends.

Bring comfort then, and courage. Strangers, friends,
Are we not all parents when children die?
What justice is, nobody comprehends.
It is the death of children most offends.

The Blue Butterfly

On my Jew's hand, born out of ghettos and shtetls,
Raised from unmarked graves of my obliterated people
In Germany, Latvia, Lithuania, Poland, Russia,

On my hand mothered by a refugee's daughter,
First opened in blitzed London, grown big
Through post-war years safe in suburban England,

On my pink, educated, ironical left hand
Of a parvenu not quite British pseudo gentleman
Which first learned to scrawl its untutored messages

Among Latin-reading rugby-playing militarists
In an élite boarding school on Sussex's green downs
And against the cloister walls of puritan Cambridge,

On my hand weakened by anomie, on my
Writing hand, now of a sudden willingly
Stretched before me in Serbian spring sunlight,

On my unique living hand, trembling and troubled
By this May visitation, like a virginal
Leaf new sprung on the oldest oak in Europe,

On my proud firm hand, miraculously
Blessed by the seven thousand martyred
Men and boys fallen at Kragujevac,

A blue butterfly simply fell out of the sky
And settled on the forefinger
Of my international bloody human hand.

Nada: Hope or Nothing

Like a windblown seed, not yet rooted,
Or petal from an impossible moonflower, shimmering,
Unplucked, perfect, in a clear night sky,

Like a rainbow without rain, like the invisible
Hand of a god stretching out of nowhere
To shower joy brimful from Plenty's horn,

Like a greeting from a child, unborn, unconceived,
Like an angel, bearing a gift, a ring, a promise,
Like a visitation from a twice redeemed soul,

Like a silent song sung by the ghost of nobody
To an unknown, sweet and melodious instrument
Buried ages in the deepest cave of being,

Like a word only half heard, half remembered,
Not yet fully learned, from a stranger's language,
The sad heart longs for, to unlock its deepest cells,

A blue butterfly takes my hand and writes
In invisible ink across its page of air
Nada, Elpidha, Nadezhda, Esperanza, Hoffnung.

There is scant hope

There is scant hope. Yet courage still there is
To thread love through the fibres of the tree
That outspans and outlasts our histories,

And though we go the ways of twigs and berries,
Branches and leaves, and in mortality
There is scant hope, yet courage still there is,

And there's no choice but love. There never is,
Through miracle or through catastrophe
That outspans and outlasts our histories.

So we must love, despite life's treacheries,
Time's wastefulness, death's crass absurdity.
There is scant hope. Yet courage still there is

To love again. Life through our arteries
Drives love, the soul's first, purest quality
That outspans and outlasts our histories.

The lines of chance and fate are mysteries
We comprehend best when we clearly see
There is scant hope. Yet courage still there is
That outspans and outlasts. Our history's.

Clean out the house

Clean out the house for springtime. Sweep the floor
In patience and in conscientiousness.
Let in the wind that's hammering at the door.

Who knows, some day we'll hammer out a cure
For cruelty, corruption, cowardice,
Clean out the house for springtime, sweep the floor,

Create a pattern, not caricature
Of natural justice, without prejudice,
Let in the wind that's hammering at the door.

But human suffering? Don't be so sure.
In practice every theory goes amiss.
Clean out the house for springtime. Sweep the floor.

We go the way the flies go. Dust, manure
Or ashes will be all that's left of us.
Let in the wind that's hammering at the door.

We can trust nothing, nowhere rest secure
Except in love, for love is limitless.
Clean out the house for springtime. Sweep the floor.
Let in the wind that's hammering at the door.

Statement by a Survivor

For Zygmunt Bauman

The too expensive treat
And the long distance call,
Beauty passed by on the street
And the pinnacle too tall
For ever hope to climb,
Remind us time and time
Again we aren't as good
Or daring as we would
Most definitely prefer
To be, or wish we were.

The banned or censored book
Wrung, certainly, from pain,
Or the frank sexual look
Of a stranger on the train
In whose beseeching eyes
We're forced to recognise
What we've imagined as
Closed or forbidden, has
For us the strongest pull,
Being inaccessible.

Whatever moves and lives,
Sweetest when out of reach,
Throws false alternatives
On the one path we each
Have no choice but to take,
Unravel, then remake,
Yet perfumes lost on wind
Still linger in the mind
And go on taking tolls
From our trawling souls.

Our brothers have gone down
Underneath the hill
With emperor and clown
As we in our time will,
Audience and spectator,
Player, referee,
Democrat, dictator,
Shareholder, employee,
Pupil and professor,
Sinner and confessor.

Because our being's cone
Narrows like a funnel
And each of us, alone,
Must go down through the tunnel,
Can even strength of kin
With all of life begin
To guide us through this maze
No bloody hope can raise
To common property
Of truth or liberty?

Though kinship with the living
as attempt or proven fact
And honestly forgiving
Are things we should not act
Or breathe or live without,
Being firm enough
Even for preaching about,
The less substantial stuff
Of fellowship with the dead
Fills us with fear and dread.

Though all we desire consists
Of impossibilities,
And though the dream persists
And without hope this is
A mad unholy feast
For liar, fool or priest,
And though no dream alone
Built Ithaca or Zion
On the pillow of a stone,
It's still desire we lie on.

As children once we dreamed
We would live for ever
And every small trick seemed
Key to some endeavour
Or adventure we'd be in
As hero, heroine.
When seas blew through our shell
We knew all would be well
And all we dreamed of would
Be achieved in adulthood.

Though we who breathe and live
Our small time on this ground
Forget but can't forgive,
Still must our dead surround
Us all with constant flame,
And pass out keys or clues
And prompt us with their cues,
And traces we cannot name
Of memory and desire
Consume us in their fire.

Nothing is lost always

Nothing is lost always. Nor do things repeat themselves
Identically, like a train or bus timetable,
Daily or seasonally. Each journey is different.
Last time, there you sat, embedded in whatever memory
Of other interiors, of yesterday night, of childhood,
Staring out of the window, probably seeing nothing,
Unaware whether you woke or were still afloat on dream.
This time, look, there's a fisherman, knee-deep in a pond,
A fox, silhouetted, loping over a hill brow,
An air-tailed mallard dipping his head in a stream
Or a field greening or yellowed, speckled with poppies.
And next time, who will you be, other than another,
Drinking at the station bar with some fellow traveller,
Swapping jokes and anecdotes, gossiping and laughing,
Or swilling alone, inside your own reflection?

When the face you know or believe you know best
Changes imperceptibly each time you examine it
Curiously, in the mirror, why your discomfort,
And if not curious, why did you look at all?
If, now and then, time moves like an indifferent clock,
It is not so always. Time too changes time. One day
Is a rich chaos unlike any other, the sun never rises
In quite the same place as yesterday or tomorrow,
Earth deviates on its axis, pulled by vanishing stars,
The carpet of galaxies moves away under your feet
While you still stand upon it – and the one face of the other
You love, and will love always, is always the other face
Of the only one you love. And that face too changes
Even as you gaze. Time too changes time, like a face,
From flatness to dimension, haze to definition,
Indifference to difference, humanity, height, depth – soul.
And as a surface changes to a face, unique, known, loved,
Although wholly other, always wholly other,

And as a loved face may be entered, understood and known,
Even if, when it happens, you cannot quite believe it,
So time's innermost fountain renews itself, murmuring,
Splashing you with its language of hidden glyphs and icons,
Music of impossibilities, constantly calling: Listen,
Take me in, drink me, and sometimes entering you too,
Spreading drops on your hands, feeding your mouth with words,
Unclasping your throat in song's affirmation and harmony,
Like a blue butterfly. And the river of sound it forms,
Flowing one way, always, then back on itself, then on,
Is incapable of revealing anything more or other
Than this, this, this. Nothing is lost always.
So learn from the clock-face, patience, until the flood
May be dived in, or gather you up like a whirlpool,
Eradicating time. Memory, my treasure, only this you ensure,
Darling I keep losing and finding again in the loss,
In cloud, evening, sunset, light flecks on water,
The solitary magpie's winged arc across an entire sky,
Leaves, animal eyes, in whatever is closest to death,
For which, in paying nothing, we pay all we have and are –
Even when you deceive, and always as miraculous
Whenever you arrive, as this butterfly on my hand
And its sounding of dead voices I do not understand
How I understand. What, then, is love, but quality
Of attention to details, to surfaces, and tracing
In them the depths you may call understanding
Of history, which moving ever forwards, curls and coils
Back on itself, as serpentine, graceful, merciless,
Resisting interpretation, and losing nothing always
As the flight of this imago, time changing time?

The Mirror

Said the garden to the sky,
You are the one book I live by.

Said the raincloud to the land,
Here is my gift. Open your hand.

Replied the earth, Although I'm blind,
Never mind, Never mind.

And while the sun and stars span round,
Seeds groaned under ground,

Singing, Grow we will and must
Till we break earth's crust.

Then a voice from heaven spoke
And all the sleeping creatures woke.

And two white birds with wide wing span
Flew in the hearts of woman and man.

And the woman stood and said,
Earth and sky join in my head.

I mirror them. They mirror me.
Through my eyes may the whole world see.

And the man knelt down and prayed
And said, From star dust we are made.

Croft Woods

To Peter Russell

I pace Croft Woods beneath a slanted source
Of sunlight by a winding river bank.
I stoop, observing mushrooms, mosses, ferns,
And trace their whorls or veins, thickened by rain.
An early autumn afternoon in England,
Green, deep and crisp, entirely beautiful.

Swifts wheel before migration. Their screams
Beckon to their companions – *Africa*!
Massed cells of blackberries hover on their bushes,
And the ground is strewn with husks, like little mines
Bobbing on an irregular green sea,
Splitting out conkers, polished to perfection.

The light here hangs diagonally down,
An alphabet of traceries and shadows
I have not learned, but only half intuit.
Illiterate, I stumble like a foreigner
Who cannot read the simplest of its messages.
But still it daunts me, calls me deep into it.

Blue moss, moonwort, fronded maidenhair,
Dusty spores of buckler and hart's tongue nestling
Under cow-grass and nettles, where I tread,
Cry for release: *Go soft now and in peace.*
I wish I were a ghost, not to disturb
Their roots planted more deeply than our dead.

I thought I heard a rising breeze above
Brush leaves, pluck branches – yes, the usual
English lute – Dowland's, Wyatt's, Shakespeare's,
Scores so well-known, familiar and loved
No repetition or variant ever could
Dull those clear chords against their bowls of wood.

But no, I stop and catch my deepening breath.
Complete silence, or silence magnified,
Full of no sound, as in a cave or well,
And I am falling into it, down, down.
I am transparent, empty, bodiless,
The instant past an echo's tadpole-tip –

The second after sound has lost its grip
On sound's reverberation, the exact moment
A tap has been turned off and stops its drip,
Or lips are closed and eyes are sealed for ever
And the heart's metronome has petered out,
Like sap in winter – all I was has vanished.

I am a shell without a listening child
To hear the sea in. I'm the sea itself
Solidified, without a moon to pull
A wind or raise a cloud or comb a wave.
Where have I gone – where has my own self gone
Out of this everlasting-seeming pause?

I stop and start. And suddenly a swelling
Of light behind the day, from day anterior
To light that patterns traceries in eyes,
Pours upwards and outswells itself, then cracks
This early evening silence like an eggshell
And a new creature hatches, out of nothing.

Like a waterfall which shatters into droplets,
A music, if it can be called a music,
As if upon a screen that is no screen
Throws images that cannot be imagined,
And I'm compelled to listen to another
Stranger, eerier music from the forest.

Our speech is built on spirals spun of air,
Voice-pillars that support whole architectures
Of meanings on their shoulders, caryatids
Without whose weight the topless roofs of thought
Would crumble and cave in, as mountains might
Be one with valleys, on the Day of Judgement.

But in the forest, mother of cathedrals,
In starred, sky-tented glade, in cultured garden,
In orchard, copse or grove, high moor or fen,
Curtains dividing speech and silence fall,
And colloquies of oxygen and carbon
Counterpoint chants of plants and breaths of men.

And these translucent symphonies of sap
Print negatives of speech, gaps, absences,
Unstitching and unweaving human voices
To dim inverted echoes of our origins,
As shimmering escarpments, cliffs and peaks
Reflect in lakes through which the abyss speaks.

On still lake surfaces lie twin perspectives,
Both open simultaneously to view:
What seems, reflected by superior light,
And all that really lives and moves below.
So, in the fugues of plants we trace both bright
Marks of our own world, and a more mysterious glow –

Less than an echo's ripple, or the gleam
On eddying water, or light-filament
Suddenly dew-decked on a spider's thread,
As if made of another element
Spun out, unbroken for us, by the dead,
And stretched to waking from behind the dream.

Now, as from mist that rises when the sun
Has dried a level band above the dawn,
A veil is drawn back through me and I wait
For it to billow wide and stretch till torn.
Which way? To climb? To dive? *My child, come down!*
I enter in. I do not hesitate.

Unbearable polyphonies! I'm hemmed
On all sides by a shadow-orchestra
Playing not sound, but mirrorings of sound,
An anti-music, music's twin and opposite,
Fluid in meanings, filled with coded messages
Of bodiless bodies, dry dews, airless airs.

Through punning alien non-calls from green stems
They challenge me in murmurs, less than murmurs
Untraceable, from the other side of silence,
Mysteriously forcing upwards through this ground
Orders to stop, to listen, and to stand
Chilled by their winds on sounds that have no sound.

Tougher than taproots, lacier than branches,
This music bids me recognise the innumerable
Dead, who stretch up moistly pleading hands
Towards me, beckoning, taunting me to enter
Through scented lips and fingertips of plants
Their watery realm of uncreated gardens.

Come down, come down, protected from the wind
That howls over the world from dusk till dawn.
Surround yourself with music underpinned
By currents in the earth, not of this air.
Pass, through the gates of ivory and horn,
Unchained alike from hope, fear and despair.

Come down, come down, beneath the plough and furrow
Where no bat dives and spider never clambers,
To wreathe old skulls in webs or nest in marrow
Under memorial slabs or tombstone lids.
Come roam our tunnelled corridors and chambers
Carved deeper far than cores of pyramids.

Come, be the dragon, vigilant through sleep,
Who guards the dungeon-treasure in the keep,
A carpenter locked in damp airless rooms
Whose roof-rafters are coffins, attics graves,
Come and be sentry to these catacombs,
The minotaur of labyrinthine caves.

Here is a music culled from peat and loam
In swamp or marsh, and hollows under hills
Where skulls of slaves and outlaws have been tossed.
Here is a score penned under frozen taiga
Where mammoth bones are packed in permafrost
Alongside undiscovered minerals.

And listening to this music is descending
A ladder dangling in an endless void,
To reach its end, let go, and still to tumble
Throughout one's self until all self is blown
Like breath from dying lungs or a balloon,
And further fall, a meteoric stone.

Deeper than self entirely, made transparent,
The dreamer enters unsleep, a new zone,
And in so doing, *climbs*! If this is falling,
It is a falling upwards, a dawn breaking
A dream undreamed, redressed, a double-waking,
And through fear so far gone, fear is unknown.

Frail leaf, veined with shadow-blood, now I touch you,
I become other, unspeaking, I grow down
Into your zone of no-time, before time-was,
Pay my obol entry to join your dream-cast,
And recall formless forms from which this world's
Definitive solid shapes are sculpted statues.

I touch a world inside the veins of rock
Which Michelangelo knew before he chiselled
To dig from them his perfect Rondanini.
I trace the clouded face of the Madonna,
I'm Goethe's Faust, descending, past the Mothers,
And the stone-carver of Dolní Vestoníce.

I fall to before Adam. Is this sleep?
No serpent in the grass can do me harm.
My child, come deeper inwards. Do not weep.
I hibernate with squirrels under snows.
I am at one with Keats and Mandelstam,
I am the bloodless blood inside the rose.

I follow tracks of grubs and centipedes,
I burrow tunnels hewn by humble worms,
I shrink or swell with water, among seeds;
My world is made of tubers, bulbs and corms,
Surrounded by their strings, drums, bells and horns
Under green mossy banks and grassy lawns.

Shall I root, like the cone of a sequoia
And grow, encircled by a ring of daughters,
And when I am a henge of dusky coal,
And milky sap's solidified in amber,
Turn fossil carbon back to living wood
Where bees, extinct, make honey from dead flowers?

And now, I have the key – of songs perpetual
Accompaniments to our own human music,
In ebbing undertow and swelling currents
Reaching deeper beneath than birds above,
More various than blackbird, thrush or field-lark,
Or nightingale's outpourings in dark gardens.

Here is the score, and now I have the words –
Prelude, crescendo, finale, strewn from silences
That lie behind dumb sources of the wind.
This song of plants builds tuned keys for the chords,
Threads to the maze, and figures to the dance,
Scales to the stars – and scaffolds to mortality.

These boughs and trunks are valves the underworld
Allows the dead we tread on underfoot
To breathe a little through from atmospheres
Funnelled from earthy moistures. Each porous
Bulb, root, tuber is a well sprung door
Hinged between death and life and keyed by dream.

Withstanding stresses higher than our hopes,
Through hollowed pipes which subtly coil and bend
On stems stretched taut, to analyse and parse
Galactic grammars without start or end,
Blossoms and flowers, like astral telescopes,
In petalled bowls snatch impulses from stars.

Is this the way for sure? I cannot know
But trust and follow one direction, down,
Deepening through darkness. There, may another light,
Agleam, then brightening like a shooting star
Shattered on ruffled waters of pale lake
Through this world's clouded margins, break and shine.

Though rainbows, ribboned evenings, arrowed twilights
And orchestras of summer afternoons
In greeny plaited mazes wreathe light hours
And blind me to that ever-other kingdom,
Still may these voices wake me, interwoven
Through trees and shrubs, with scents of herbs and flowers.

As for the birds that wheel among upon these trees
Surrounding me, and call to their companions,
They'll be my questioned questioners, not masters.
My frank inquisitors, and testers of my spirit.
We shall migrate like them, on beating air,
And suddenly be no longer anywhere.

What love I bear you, world, I cannot vow
To promises, allurements, wedding rings
Of human projects cast in mere futurities.
If love is to be filled it must be now
By trusting in the heights *and* depths of things.
Love cannot grow, die, be reborn. *It is.*

Mirrors of music: see how here I go
Down, inward, through impenetrable shells
Of silences, through silence, into silence.
Towers of Babel, walls of Jericho
Tumble to petalled trumpets, pollen bells
Of flowers strung on unfathomable wells.

Spectres of blossoms, cloudy petal fluff
And wind-tossed seeds thrown feathered from their husks
Play melodies that can't be tracked on air.
Chords brushed from nothing, plaited lacy stuff,
Chains out of nowhere, cables combed from void,
Join death to us across their bridge of hair.

Conundrums of falling leaves, brushed honey-gold,
Cyclamen, autumn crocus, moss and mould,
Print coded passwords on my lips that yet
Are steeped and webbed in dew, still freshly wet.
These voices call from zones where dews have dried
And guiding hope and love rest purified.

Guests

Yes, we have come for rest, so
give us, kindly, rest's instruments –
salt, bread, dried fruit, olives,
a little meat if you have it,
and a flask of local wine.
We have no needs or preferences
especially out of the ordinary,
no special news, imports, nothing
to declare or purvey. Only let
your basins be clean, cushions
freshly aired, sheets spotless
and cool, couches without vermin.
We do have our own obligations,
that is several duties and rituals
which incidentally require of us
certain minor observances –
concerning which however we really
need not trouble you. Nor shall
we dream of burdening you
with more than conventional courtesies
in thanks for your unobtrusive
kindly hospitality, and no, of course,
absolutely, no trinkets, no gifts,
no mementoes, let alone any such
subtler outlandish embarrassments
as unredeemable blessings.
We assure you we shall pack
away our utensils neatly
leaving no traces of them.
We shall rise early, pay and be gone.
Dawn's shadows will efface us
and by noon we shall have left
no ripple on the surface of memory.

Poems from *The Manager*

I will speak

I will speak. Yes I will. I will not, cannot be silenced. I am responsible for this seed landed here called Human

To root it through and through me till every pore breathes. That it break this sheen on the stuff of things

That it scratch this varnished light a little. To trace what lies beneath it. That what be called gross or foul

Be charged with clearer breath. For blood, sweat, salt are particles of radiance. And shall be known by their true names

And for what they really are. But how perfection leaks from cracks in the bowl of now. And how time

Drips constant through the porous jar of presence. And how you and I may waste, trying to fit shards together.

Yet I will speak. I must. And of these things too. This plant that grows from our speech in joy here I name: Community.

Once, hearing music

Once, hearing music, I thought: A man or woman made this. And once there was a time before its pattern was. Before its form or harmonies had ever been conceived

Out of flesh and its travails. Out of the labour of hands. And before that, a time when not one single quaver of it had been the slenderest shadow. Less even than a shadow

Lying dark in its maker. Until it was shaped, crafted and nourished into light. And he or she no angel but human to the core. Who made it for you, for me, that we

Might see clear through it, build our own work upon it, and by our willing love, also transform our world. That through us, matter be known, transparent and resplendent

As music. And with these thoughts, I rejoiced to be in its history, to be alive in its time: my time now his and hers. And yours too, as you hear this. Which is not the time its maker

Lay less than a pip in an apple, unformed, unborn, unnamed. Yet to you and me in our times that maker of music reached out. And me here humanly touched. And moved to make this.

In the parks and among the flowering gardens

In the parks and among the flowering gardens. My cousin, my sister. At this moment when the conductor of the big brass band rests his baton. At this pause steeped in quietness. At this very still point – which is yet

Not yet an ending – I pray do not come yet. For I am by no means ready. I still have things to do. For example, to call, to bear witness. To this sweet, sultry, old-new spring, now on the lilac-perfumed brink

Of spilling into summer. And to note how cunningly mingled are the stars above with cloud. Cirrus, cumulus, altostratus. Trout-speckled, mackerelled, frog-skinned. Streaked with slime, silver, promises

And countless other etceteras. So, cousin, I must beg your forgiveness. How can I not be besotted with these movements of light and shadow, these subtly flickering interplays, these textural incongruities, this chaos

Of fusings, branchings, connections, intersections? For it is the ordinary spaces most call us out to be loved. And the common imperfections that most shape surprise and miracle. And the typical idiosyncrasies that

Well up depths and desires. And by solo and chorus, repeatedly demand that we, who are growing old, once more gaze childlike through them. And each and every time, gaze, as though for the very first time.

Ah, my sister. In the parks and among the flowering gardens. Even when we have crossed over, and are fully bereft of futurity, when shall we ever be ready?

And even in that split instant, when the soul is in neither zone, neither here nor there, but hovers between, like a butterfly – *shall we ever be ready?*

Notes

The poem 'Against the Day' (pp. 11-19) is, among other things, a commentary on Jan Vermeer's painting 'The Guitar Player', which appears on the cover. The original is in Kenwood House, Hampstead. The epigraph is from Sir Edmund Spenser's 'Prothalamion'. Numerological patternings of various kinds are used in 'Against the Day', as in several other poems in this book. 'Angels', for example (pp. 44-47), has exactly 100 lines.

'Tree' (pp. 31-40) has the same number of lines as a calendar year has days. This makes it three lines longer than the height, in feet, of the tallest tree in the world, the Coast Redwood 'Howard Libbey Tree' in Humboldt State Park, California. The epigraph is from Basilides of Alexandria.

The epigraph to 'The Core' (p.23) is from Edward Thomas.

Four poems belong to a sequence entitled *Black Light*, set in Greece. The epigraphs from George Seferis, to whose memory the sequence is dedicated, are taken from his *Collected Poems*, tr. Edmund Keeley and Philip Sherrard (Princeton University Press, 1967). The title 'Volta' (p.54) means 'evening promenade' in Greek. In the same poem, 'Eleftería' (p.55) means 'freedom' and is a popular girl's name.

Eight poems are included from the unpublished sequence *The Blue Butterfly* (pp.59-70). The historical point of departure for this group of poems was a Nazi massacre of Yugoslav men and boys in the Serbian town of Kragujevac on 21st October 1941. The town and the memorial site were heavily bombed by NATO planes in 1999. Both 'The Blue Butterfly' and 'Nada: Hope or Nothing' were directly triggered by the event of a butterfly landing on my hand outside the memorial museum in Kragujevac in May 1985. 'Nada', which means 'nothing' in Spanish, at the same time means 'hope' in Serbo-Croat, and is also a popular girl's name. The last line of this poem repeats the word for 'hope' in Serbo-Croat, Greek, Russian, Spanish and German.

The final three poems, 'I will speak', 'Once, hearing music' and 'In the parks and among the flowering gardens' belong to an unpublished sequence entitled *The Manager*.

RB, Cambridge, 1999

Other King of Hearts Publications

Coming Home, by Gareth Calway, 1991
An ambitious sequence describing, in a wide variety of styles, from ballad and sonnet to free verse and Sufi ghazals, the journey of the soul through creation and human history to its final spiritual destination.
Paperback, 70pp, £4.95.

The Return of Inanna: a myth for our time, by Juliet Wimhurst, 1994
A re-telling of an ancient Sumerian myth, exploring its modern relevance, through poems and powerful black and white woodcuts.
Paperback, 50pp, 12 illustrations, £4.95.

Black Light, by Richard Burns, 1995
A sequence of poems celebrating the Greek landscape and light, and the Greek poetic tradition, written in homage to the poet George Seferis.
Paperback, 28pp, £4.95.

Odes to the King of Hearts, by Namo, 1998
A series of poems inspired by the Sufi ghazal, expressing longing for God and the trials and tribulations of a modern disciple.
Paperback, 60pp, £4.95.

These books may be ordered from
The King of Hearts Publications, Fye Bridge Street, Norwich NR3 1LJ.
Email: kingofhearts@paston.co.uk